12.95

World's Most Bone-Chilling "True" Ghost Stories

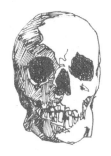

John Macklin

Illustrated by Jim Sharpe

 Sterling Publishing Co., Inc. New York

Library of Congress Cataloging-in-Publication Data

Macklin, John.
    World's most bone-chilling "true" ghost stories / by John Macklin ;
illustrated by Jim Sharpe.
        p.   cm.
    Includes index.
    Summary: A collection of twenty-four short, purportedly true
stories about ghosts, strange disappearances, and odd events from
around the world.
    ISBN 0-8069-0390-2
    1. Ghosts—Juvenile literature. [1. Ghosts. 2. Supernatural.]
I. Sharpe, Jim, ill. II. Title.
BF1461.M3389   1993
133.1—dc20   93–16616
                                              CIP
                                              AC

10 9 8 7 6 5 4 3 2 1

Published in 1993 by Sterling Publishing Company, Inc.
387 Park Avenue South, New York, N.Y. 10016
© 1993 by Sterling Publishing Company, Inc.
The text in this book has been excerpted from *Brotherhood of the Strange*
copyright © 1972 and *Dwellers in Darkness* copyright © 1968 both by Ace
Books, Inc.
Illustrations © 1993 by Jim Sharpe
Distributed in Canada by Sterling Publishing
% Canadian Manda Group, P.O. Box 920, Station U
Toronto, Ontario, Canada M8Z 5P9
Distributed in Great Britain and Europe by Cassell PLC
Villiers House, 41/47 Strand, London WC2N 5JE, England
Distributed in Australia by Capricorn Link Ltd
P.O. Box 665, Lane Cove, NSW 2066
Manufactured in the United States of America
All rights reserved

Sterling ISBN 0-8069-0390-2 Trade
              0-8069-0391-0 Paper

Contents

1. CURSES AND VENGEANCE

- A mummy case brings death to its owners.

- An island is protected by an evil guardian.

- Ancient priests won't allow *anything* to be removed from their city.

- A witch's curse is fulfilled.

When Death Comes on Swift Wings

It was a warm evening in April, 1924, and the three young men were enjoying a card game on the deck of the steamer as it sailed lazily down the River Nile.

They had not met until the voyage started, but they had so many interests in common that they were soon firm friends.

Gordon Richardson, 26, was an archæologist whose main interest was exploring the tombs of the pharaohs. After the card game, he amused his friends, Ian Grant and Philip Masters, by talking about some of his experiences. Masters jokingly mentioned the ancient curse of the pharaohs: "Death shall come on swift wings to him that defileth the tomb of a pharaoh." Wasn't Richardson worried about that, he teased. Richardson laughed and explained that he kept an open mind on these matters.

The next morning, the steamer arrived at Aswan and the trio wandered ashore to the market, where Grant was intrigued by a mummy case that an Arab trader was selling. Grant had beaten the Arab down from the equivalent of $100 to $80, when Richardson took over, speaking in rapid Arabic. Minutes later, he told the others that the price was down to $32.

As the mummy case was genuine and would easily fetch $450 in London, Richardson suggested that each of them put up $8. It would add a little spice to their card games if ownership of the mummy went to whichever one was the winner when the journey ended in Cairo.

The mummy case was taken aboard and maneuvered into the nearest cabin, Grant's.

The next morning, Grant did not turn up as usual for breakfast. When the steward went to his cabin, the only occupant was the mummy case standing unseeing in the corner.

Grant's bunk had not been slept in, and he was never heard of again. He was presumed to have fallen overboard and been drowned, but no cry for help had been heard.

Richardson and Masters were stunned by the tragedy. That evening, Richardson retired early to his cabin, where the case had been taken. When he failed to appear for breakfast the following morning, Masters went to his cabin anxiously. Richardson was in bed, but only semiconscious and suffering from fever. A few hours later he was dead. A post-mortem was carried out, but the cause of his death remained a mystery.

Masters refused pointblank to have the mummy case in his cabin, because he could not believe that the double tragedy was a coincidence. When he disembarked in Cairo, a cable was waiting to inform him that the family business had been ruined in a bank crash.

When the mummy case arrived in England, it was promptly sold, yet its history of tragedy was by no means over. Some years later, Madame Blavatsky, a celebrated clairvoyant, was invited to a large party in London. She had no sooner arrived than she announced that she was quite unable to stay in the house and had to leave immediately. There was some malevolent influence there, she said—something diabolical and harmful.

A little annoyed, the host jokingly invited her to have a look around and locate the ghost for them. Madame Blavatsky went into all the rooms without comment, but on entering the attic, she stiffened and exclaimed, "It is here. I feel it!"

She hunted around the room in semi-darkness, opened a closet in the far corner and found the mummy case. The owner of the house looked at it in astonishment. She had never seen it before as she only bought the house a week earlier, after the sudden death of the previous tenants. Madame Blavatsky had never been inside the house before or heard the history of the mummy case, but she left at once, imploring her hosts to get rid of the evil thing immediately.

Her advice was taken and the mummy case was given to the British Museum, where two porters carried it upstairs. One fell on the steps and broke his leg; the other died suddenly of a heart attack the following day.

Dr. Budge, in charge of the mummy, had a photographer take pictures of the object for a catalogue. The next day the photographer rushed out of the darkroom in great excitement to tell a fellow technician that there was something extraordinary about the photograph.

His colleague shuddered when he examined the negative beneath a light, for there was no doubt about it; there *was* a macabre-looking face leering, somehow, through the mummy case.

As there wasn't time that day to make prints, the photographer dropped in to see Dr. Budge on his way home, to tell him about the phenomenon. Budge was most anxious to see a print of the picture, so the photographer returned to his studio to make it up. That was the last time he was seen alive.

The following morning, his colleagues found the darkroom door locked from the inside. Forcing it open they found the photographer lying dead on the floor, with a cruel gash across his throat.

There was no sign of the negative or any prints that involved the mummy case. Neither was there any weapon that could have been used in the suicide—or murder.

The Witch Doctor of Pulo Jehat

The island had lain undisturbed for 100 years. Like a sentinel, it rose up from the waters of the Johore Straits, the narrow strip of sea that separates Singapore from the Malayan mainland. The natives called it Pulo Jehat—the Wicked Island.

Over the years, few had dared to set foot on it. It was cursed, they said, and protected by an evil, all-powerful guardian named Merah, who had been dead for more than a century.

A powerful witch doctor, Merah had lived alone in the middle of a mangrove swamp on what is now Singapore Island. Since, according to Malayan folklore, evil spirits are unable to cross water, when Merah died, he was buried on the little island at the eastern end of the Johore Straits.

But although Merah was dead, his evil lived on in native legends, even after the village grew into the great port of Singapore. And in 1938, when the British decided to strengthen the defenses of Singapore against a possible attack from the sea, it became evident just how deeply rooted these local superstitions were.

The British planned to set up a number of guns to guard the eastern approaches to the Johore Straits, and Pulo Jehat was the ideal site. But there was a problem: No native laborers would go near the place. Both Malay and Chinese workmen were convinced that to set foot on Pulo Jehat meant risking Merah's fury. Even an offer of double pay failed to change their minds.

At last, a Muslim priest, who lived on the neighboring island of Tekong, contacted army authorities. He said he might be able to solve the problem by visiting the island and communing with the spirit of the dead witch doctor. He would try to persuade Merah's ghost to lie low until the gun stations were completed. In view of the fearful dangers involved, he asked a small fee— $100 (£60).

The priest spent two days alone on Pulo Jehat; and when he returned, he told the authorities that Merah had "agreed" not to hinder the army's work, provided that no one disturb his tomb.

Somewhat reassured, the local laborers began work, and after six weeks the gun placements were completed. The job had gone ahead without interference, supernatural or otherwise. The army had its fortifications; the Muslim priest had earned his fee; the workers had earned their double pay. Everyone was happy—until the engineer came along.

He was a representative of the British firm that supplied the power plant for the installation. When the work was finished, he visited the island to make sure that the firm's equipment was in working order.

Even after ten years in the Far East, the engineer was convinced that superstition was a load of nonsense. And despite the entreaties of his Chinese assistant, he was determined to prove it—by spitting on Merah's tomb.

To his assistant's amazement, nothing happened. No winged demons appeared to carry off the engineer; no thunderbolt flashed out of the sky to strike him down.

But things began to go wrong.

A few hours later, one of the engineer's staff, a Chinese mechanic, had the fingers of his right hand sliced off by the fan of a diesel engine's watercooler.

Then the electricity generators on the island stopped working for no apparent reason. The diesel engines that powered them were still running perfectly, and there was nothing to account for the sudden failure.

The next morning the generators hummed to life without a hitch. They continued to work perfectly for another month, and then the power failed again. This time, the fault was traced to the heavy, lead-covered cables that ran across the island from the generator building to the gun positions.

At the exact spot where the cables passed Merah's tomb, their protective lead covering had flaked away like dry clay.

The lead was renewed, and the equipment gave no more trouble. But within a week, the curse of Merah struck again. A piece of equipment fell out of a boat that was being unloaded on Pulo Jehat, and a Malay coolie dived into the sea to recover it.

Seconds later, he was dead—his lower body crushed in the jaws of a shark.

One Japanese pilot tried to bomb the gun positions on the island. His bomb missed its target, and the gunners below watched as the bomber continued its dive. It was not damaged in any way—yet the pilot seemed frozen at the controls. The plane smacked into the sea and blew up.

The engineer who had spat on Merah's tomb escaped from Singapore just a few hours before the Japanese captured the city. He was lucky—or so it seemed at first.

But three months later, his eyesight began to fail. Eye specialists were completely baffled, but there was nothing they could do. Eventually, he went totally blind.

Since then, Merah has been left to rest in peace.

Curse of the Old Ones

Just north of Mombasa, where the Indian Ocean rolls gently against Kenya's 250-mile-long coastline, lies the ancient city of Gedi. A crumbling ruin, overgrown with creepers, it has been abandoned for centuries. No one knows who lived there, or why they left, and no native will go near the place.

But this is not just because of the snakes and poisonous creeping creatures that infest the city. According to local legend, Gedi is guarded by the "Old Ones"—the spirits of priests who once ruled the temple and promised to protect the ruins throughout eternity. It's easy to believe this legend, because Gedi is veiled by an uncanny silence, and huge trees spread their canopies over the ruins as if to enfold countless dark mysteries.

Some years ago, an English tourist named Jack Bateson was attracted by the legends that surrounded Gedi. As he was something of an artist, he thought that the ruins, particularly the ancient temple, would make a good subject for a painting.

When Bateson told his native guide what he planned to do, the man was horrified and begged him not to go. The Old Ones wrought a terrible vengeance, the guide said, on anyone rash enough to remove anything from their home. And they would surely never forgive anyone taking away an image of their sacred temple in the form of a painting!

Bateson laughed. He didn't believe in spirits, and what harm could there be in painting a picture of what, after all, was nothing more than a crumbling ruin?

The next day he loaded his painting materials and a picnic lunch into his car and set out for Gedi, accompanied by his wife and two daughters.

It turned out to be a splendid day. It was cool beneath the trees, and Bateson had seldom felt so relaxed. Only once, about three o'clock in the afternoon, did anything strange happen. Bateson was sketching the old temple when he saw—or *thought* he saw—a white-robed figure flitting among the trees. None of the others had seen the apparition, so Bateson shrugged the matter off, dismissing it as a trick of the light. Nevertheless, he couldn't shake off a feeling of unease.

Twilight fell quickly, and suddenly the ruins took on a sinister appearance. Bateson felt a peculiar wave of tiredness sweep over him, and with it came an overpowering urge to flee from the place as quickly as possible.

The feeling vanished as soon as Bateson and his family were on the road back to Mombasa—and, strangely, he found that he was driving in brilliant sunshine. Dusk had touched the ruins long before it crept over the rest of the area!

Still, the time spent at Gedi had been rewarding, because the pictures and sketches were among the best he had ever done. The next day he showed his painting of the ancient temple to a friend, who immediately offered to buy it. Impulsively, Bateson *gave* him the picture as a parting gift, since the Batesons were returning to England in a few days' time.

Back home, immersed in the everyday routine of work, Bateson forgot about Gedi. He didn't give the Old Ones or the legend a thought—not even when he fell downstairs and broke his leg a few weeks later.

He was hardly on his feet again when there was another accident. This time the victim was his eldest daughter, who broke an ankle playing hockey.

Then his wife slashed her hand badly with a pair of garden shears.

Bateson told himself that these were just unfortunate coincidences. Then a letter arrived from his friend in Mombasa—the one to whom he had given the painting. To his horror, Bateson learned that his friend's family had experienced a similar catalogue of accidents.

Bateson felt strangely compelled to return to Kenya. As soon as his work permitted, he flew to Mombasa, leaving his family in England and taking his pictures of Gedi with him. The morning after his arrival he was leaving his hotel when he met the native guide who had first warned him not to go to Gedi.

"I knew you would return," the African said. "It is well, for you have very little time. The Old Ones will not wait much longer. There is only one thing to do—you must burn the paintings."

Slowly, Bateson returned to his room. He had made up his mind: the Old Ones had to be appeased. It would break his heart, but he would destroy the paintings.

His sad task completed, Bateson hired a car and drove to his friend's house. The man greeted him warmly, but looked pale and ill. Bateson urged him to destroy the painting of the ruined temple, which was hanging over the mantelpiece. The man laughed incredulously and flatly refused, saying that the painting was one of his most treasured possessions. Nothing Bateson said or did could change his mind.

Bateson flew back to England. The curse of the Old Ones seemed to have been lifted; he had no more accidents.

Less than a month later, he learned that his friend, together with his entire family, had been killed in a car crash.

The Curse of the Witches of Skye

A cold, wintry gale was howling outside, as Margaret Fraser lay on the couch in front of the peat fire in the cottage where she and her husband, Norman, lived on the west coast of Scotland's Isle of Skye. It was December, 1900.

Margaret was expecting her fourth child, and since her husband, a shepherd, was out on the hillside, Mrs. Mackinnon, a neighbor, had come in to help tend the youngest of the Frasers' three children, Morag, a little girl about a year old.

Both women were drowsy. Soon Mrs. Mackinnon nodded off, lulled by the warmth of the glowing peat fire.

Margaret Fraser was almost asleep too, when she heard a low muttering. She opened her eyes and saw three ugly little old women sitting around the fire, whispering together, as they admired the sleeping child. They were certainly not women from the neighborhood. Then Margaret suddenly understood: these were no ordinary visitors. They were witches who had come to harm the baby.

Margaret pretended to sleep while one of the hags got up, reached out for the child, and said to the others: "We will take her away and leave at once."

The other two disagreed. "You have so many from this house already," countered one. "Better instead to put a curse on her."

So the first witch cast a spell.

"When this sod of peat shall burn away, that child shall die and go to clay." And she hurled a piece of peat into the fire.

Then the witches vanished. Margaret rose quickly from her couch, took the piece of peat from the fire and extinguished it in a pail of water. Then, wrapping the peat in a rag, she locked it away in a chest and hoped that she had beaten the awful curse.

The chest and its dreadful secret remained a mystery in the family for more than 20 years. Morag, the baby girl, grew up to be a beautiful young woman who eventually became engaged to a handsome young man.

It was the custom in the islands in those days that an engaged girl did not attend church from the day of her betrothal until the day of her marriage.

So one Sunday, while her parents attended church, Morag felt more tempted than ever to have a look in the old chest that her mother always kept locked and hidden in the cupboard.

She found a screwdriver and forced it open. She saw

nothing unusual inside, except a piece of charred peat, wrapped in a rag.

She couldn't imagine what possessed her mother to keep a piece of peat so carefully concealed in a chest. She had never heard it spoken of in the family.

Morag could not think of any better use for the piece of peat than to toss it on the fire.

No sooner had the peat begun to burn than the girl grew afraid. She was seized with a strange feeling that something was going to happen to her.

Meanwhile, Morag's parents were making their way home from church. As they walked they heard an oystercatcher down by the shore crying, "Kleep-kleep." This bird, when in flight, looks like a black-and-white cross. Its melancholy cry was taken as a warning of imminent disaster.

Getting nearer home, the Frasers heard their dog whining anxiously and saw the animal running around the house, obviously excited. They ran to the cottage.

Inside they found Morag. She was dying from no visible cause. There was no sign of the peat that the witches had cursed more than 20 years before. It had burned to nothing. The fate that Morag had been saved from in her infancy had caught up with her at last.

2. MURDER LIVES ON!

- A murder takes place in the mirror—and out.

- Two murdered men take their gruesome revenge.

- They called it Spook House—and for good reason!

Death in a Dark Mirror

Max Hellier was never able to explain exactly what it was that woke him from his normally deep sleep. He could usually sleep through any disturbance.

The room was pitch-black, and although there was no light of any sort from the window, a faint, bluish glimmer permeated the gloom. It was a weird pulsating reflection of light, unlike any Hellier had ever seen.

Then he noticed that the light was surrounding the reflection of the bedroom door in the mirror on the opposite wall. But it was something else that almost made his heart stop beating. For although he could see nobody beside him in the bed, a quick glance to the side showed a definite indentation of the pillow and the outline of a body beneath the blankets.

Even worse, there was a sudden intense coldness beside him—almost as if he were lying beside a corpse! He glanced in the mirror again and stifled a scream of horror. Hellier couldn't see *himself* reflected in the dark mirror, but there was another man lying there—a burly, bearded, handsome man with a swarthy complexion. And at that instant, Hellier could *hear* the man's heavy breathing.

Then—still in the mirror—he saw the bedroom door open slowly and a woman peer in. Her eyes were fixed on the figure of the bearded man on the bed.

Hellier watched as she crept up to the man with a horrible, feline stealth and grip the sleeper's throat with her long, bony fingers. He stared silently at the mirror as she squeezed the last breath of life from the hefty man. Then suddenly the hideous drama ended. The picture faded and Hellier was once more alone in the room.

Badly shaken by this experience, Hellier wished he had stayed somewhere else. He had disliked the room in the inn in Munich as soon as he saw it, especially the tall mirror that overshadowed the room, reflecting every movement, every tiny disturbance. Hellier, like many people, never slept on the left side of his bed, and now, as he sat shivering in the huge bed, staring at the empty mirror, he was grateful for his habit of sleeping on the right. He sank thankfully back onto the pillows and tried to blot the dreadful vision of murder from his mind.

In the morning, he was sure that he had either dreamed the incident or else that his tired brain had run riot. He would have left the inn that very day except that he met an old army buddy walking through

Munich. Franz Braun was down on his luck. His heart had always been in painting, but Hellier knew he had little talent. Braun had no job, no money, and that very morning had been evicted from his lodgings.

Hellier offered Braun a meal at the inn and a night's lodging—not only out of friendship. Hellier wanted to see if Braun too would see the strange scene in the mirror!

It turned out that now, in 1952, Braun had changed little from his war days. He wined and dined lavishly on Hellier's money and spent the whole evening flirting with the barmaid.

Hellier had already gone up to the room when Braun came bustling in.

"She had to get back to work," he told Hellier, "so we may as well turn in for the night."

Hellier nodded.

Braun said, "The girl warned me not to sleep on the left side of the bed. I wonder why."

Hellier had not told Braun about the apparitions in the mirror, but Braun was skeptical anyway about supernatural experiences. They settled down to sleep, Braun on the left side of the bed.

It was hours later when Hellier woke to find that the room was deadly cold and, in the mirror at the foot of the bed, the bedroom door glowed again with that ghostly light.

He stared at the reflection. There was no sign of himself or Braun in the mirror, but the form of the heavy, dark-skinned man was once more lying on the left-hand side. Hellier turned to look at the form beside him, but the face on the pillow was that of Franz Braun.

Hellier looked back to the mirror, and just as it had

on the previous night, the door in the mirror opened slowly. The same gaunt, marble-like face peered in and, with brutish determination, the figure crept towards the bed, its face contorted with malice. The cruel white fingers settled once more on the throat beneath the man's bushy beard.

Hellier watched fascinated as the woman's hands clasped tighter and tighter. Then, as the shuddering form in the mirror grew still, both figures vanished.

Braun had not stirred at all during the drama, but now Hellier turned to his friend and shook him. Braun could not be roused. Alarmed, Hellier snapped on the light, and then he let out a cry of sheer terror.

Braun was dead. On his throat were two red marks, slowly fading from sight.

Hellier's scream roused everybody. The doctor who was called attributed Braun's death to heart failure, but Hellier knew that Braun had been as healthy as a young horse.

The next day he questioned the barmaid, who had warned Braun about sleeping on the left-hand side of the bed. The girl looked at him uncertainly before saying, "I was right to warn him, Herr Hellier. The last few people who slept on the left side of that bed died in exactly the same way . . ."

The Violent Souls of Two Murdered Men

In the rapidly growing city of Sydney, New South Wales, at the turn of the century, few men were more respected than George Woodfall. His bluff, hearty manner was typical of the "digger" he had been 20 years before when a lucky gold strike had made his fortune.

Then suddenly on March 3, 1901, he disappeared. Nothing was missing from his luxurious house, and there was no sign of foul play. Woodfall had simply vanished into the immensity of the Australian continent, and the Sydney police registered another "missing person."

But George Woodfall was to be heard from again—in circumstances so horrible that witnesses were to doubt their own sanity.

Four years later, in October, the Reverend Charles Power and his friend William Rowley were camping in the mountains of Australia's Great Dividing Range. They pitched their tent by a stream near a waterfall that thundered down the cliff face.

The spot seemed ideal, but Father Power began to feel a sense of impending evil. Glancing at his companion, he saw that Rowley was feeling it too.

Suddenly, the sky darkened. Black clouds blocked the warm glow of the setting sun, and a huge clap of thunder burst over the mountains. In the silence that followed, the roar of the waterfall seemed ominous.

As they watched, shivering with a nameless fear,

Power gripped Rowley's arm. He could not speak, but gestured up towards the curtain of spray that hung around the waterfall. Through the crashing torrent, breaking the curtain of black water, a human hand was reaching out to the two men!

A human hand—but the hand of a corpse! Tightly stretched, the brown, withered skin writhed over flesh-less bones. As the two men watched, another hand came into view—then the arms of the thing—and they too were withered and obscene.

In Father Power's own words: "A human figure came into sight. A figure, rather, that had been human—once. Now . . . a ghastly parody of life.

"The awful thing writhed and twisted in what seemed a frenzied dance, now standing erect, now falling to knees that were no more than rough knobs of bone.

"At last . . . I tore my eyes from the terrible, tormented thing . . . praying that I might not be insane. When, at last, I looked again—the apparition had vanished."

The two men passed a sleepless night. At daybreak taking lanterns, they scrambled up the cliff to the spot where they had seen the awful figure. There, as they had half-expected and half-feared, they found a cave leading behind the waterfall.

Power led the way along a broad path leading into the mountainside. They came to a large inner cave from which a smaller chamber, cut into the rock, opened. "Suddenly," he recounted, "a wave of terror swept over me."

An open grave yawned in front of them. It had been dug years before, for the soil thrown up on either side was caked hard. On each side of the dreadful pit sat a skeleton.

The two men stepped forward and peered into the grave. There lay another body. It had the shrivelled mummified face of the apparition in the waterfall.

Its hands were clasped around a small metal box. Inside was a yellowed sheet of paper—the last confession of George Woodfall, the man who had disappeared four years before.

It made grim reading. Woodfall told how he had murdered his two partners in a dispute over their gold claim, the very claim that had established his fortune. Woodfall had dragged the bodies to the cave behind the waterfall and returned to Sydney, sole owner of the gold strike.

Twenty years passed. Then one night in March, Woodfall was awakened by a voice. It said, simply. "We shall expect you tomorrow."

It was the 20th anniversary of the murders—and Woodfall knew that he must return to the cave.

The confession ended: "When this confession is placed in the hands of the authorities, then my tortured soul may find peace at last."

Before they left, Powers and Rowley took the shovel that lay in the cave and widened the grave, burying the two skeletons, together with the remains of George Woodfall.

They handed Woodfall's confession over to the Sydney police, but to their dying day, Power and Rowley refused to disclose the whereabouts of the cave. "The violent souls," said Power, "should be left to seek peace at last."

The place has never been found.

Spook House

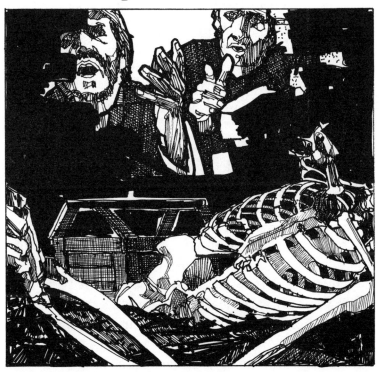

It had once been known as Spook House, the old building in Hydesville, Massachusetts. But the children playing there in November of 1904 had no thought of legends or ghosts, and it was a complete surprise when part of one wall suddenly collapsed. One of the children was practically buried. The others ran for help, and the owner of the house, William Hyde, and others went to the rescue.

They freed the child and then noticed that there was a hole between the fallen wall and the cellar foundation. In the hole they found a peddler's tin box and close to it the incomplete skeleton of a man. The head was missing.

This evidence settled once and for all a controversy that had raged in the previous century when a family named Fox lived there. They had claimed they experienced weird, ghostly happenings. Their story is one of the most fantastic occult tales of all time.

John Fox, a farmer, lived in the hamlet of Hydesville with his wife and two daughters, Margaretta, 13, and Catherine, 9.

They were a highly respected family, and until they moved into the house in 1848, their life was quiet and unexciting. Then it started. They began to hear inexplicable tapping noises, sometimes soft, sometimes very loud, as if heavy objects were being moved around. Both children became so frightened that their bed had to be moved into their parents' room. Then, the ghostly rappings became so loud and so violent that the beds shook as if an earthquake were rocking them.

The family searched the house, but could find no explanation. The ghostly tapping became progressively louder. Soon the family was completely worn out from lack of sleep.

One night when the noises began, nine-year-old Catherine clapped her hands and challenged the ghost to imitate her. At once her claps were repeated.

Then Mrs. Fox asked the spirit to tap out the ages of her children. To their amazement, the ghost immediately obliged. It even paused for a couple of seconds and then rapped out "three." A third child had died at the age of three.

Joining her daughter, Mrs. Fox asked the spirit to signal with two knocks if it was indeed a spirit, and there followed almost at once two distinct taps. Growing more confident, Mrs. Fox put more questions to the ghost, indicating the number of taps to be given for each specific answer.

In this way, she learned that the spirit was a man who had been murdered when he was 31, and that his body was buried in the cellar of the house. A neighbor, Mr. Duesler, put questions to the ghost, and learned that the killing had been carried out in a bedroom some five years earlier, with a butcher knife, and that not until the night following the murder was the body taken down into the cellar, to be buried 10 feet under the floor of the house.

The spirit also rapped out the information that the killer had been motivated by robbery, stealing $500 from the victim. The cellar was dug up, but nothing was unearthed. This caused many people to accuse the Fox family of manufacturing the whole story.

The following summer, digging was restarted and this time evidence was found—traces of quicklime and charcoal, a plank, hairs, and pieces of bone that a doctor declared had come from a human skull. But no body was found.

Then came more unexpected evidence to support the Fox family's story. Lucretia Pulver, who had been employed as a servant by the former tenants, a Mr. and Mrs. Bell, said that one day a peddler, aged about 30, had called at the house. She had seen him talking with Mrs. Bell, who claimed the man was an old acquaintance.

Lucretia was dismissed by Mrs. Bell that same day, but before she left, she asked the peddler to call at her home before leaving the district, because she wished to buy something from him. He agreed to stop by the next morning, but he never did.

A few days later, she was amazed to be offered her job back by Mrs. Bell. Returning to the house, she saw Mrs. Bell altering some coats, and several things from the peddler's pack were lying around the house.

Sent down to the cellar one evening, Lucretia fell on loose earth. She screamed and Mr. Bell proceeded to fill in what he told her were rat holes.

Lucretia also reported other strange happenings— ghostly rappings and other mysterious sounds. Soon after this, the Bells left the house.

Lucretia's story threw suspicion on Bell, but he was never charged, there being no definite evidence against him.

After the Fox family left, no one went to live in Spook House again.

3. WHAT'S OUT THERE?

- A plane is slammed out of the sky—as if by a giant hand.

- Sound waves terrorize an English village.

- Young Michael Norton disappears without a trace.

- Spirits of the dead surround an old man and terrorize a hospital staff.

A Deadly Game of
Cat and Mouse

At 6:30 on the evening of April 1, 1959, a big four-engined C-118 transport aircraft of the USAF's 175th Air Transport Wing roared down the main runway of McChord Air Force Base, near Tacoma, Washington, and climbed into the southern sky. For the four men on board, this was a routine training mission—so routine that it was virtually automatic.

At 7:45 P.M. the staff in the control tower at McChord Air Force Base heard a frantic distress call from the C-118's pilot. "Mayday! Mayday! We've hit something—or something has hit us! I am returning to base." Then, a few seconds later came a final, desperate scream:

"This is it! This is it!" And then there was only silence.

The C-118 had crashed into the side of a mountain in the Cascade Range, 30 miles northwest of Mount Rainier's 14,400-foot peak. Air Force crash crews and armed guards raced to the scene. Newsmen and others who attempted to get close were warned off at gunpoint. Explanations and rumors spread like wildfire: had the aircraft been testing some new device? That was unlikely, since the C-118 was only a freighter. Could pilot error be the answer? Or perhaps the C-118 had run into a flock of birds, or collided with another plane? Then—why the secrecy?

But the Air Force knew that none of these reasons was the real one, because a few minutes before the pilot's distress call, the powerful radar at McChord Air Force Base had revealed that the C-118 had picked up three or four mysterious travelling companions—strange, luminous specks of light that darted around the big transport. Gradually, the Air Force specialists who were investigating the crash had built up a minute-by-minute picture of the strange and terrifying fate of the large aircraft.

At seven o'clock on that April evening, residents in the area between Seattle and Mount Rainier had been alarmed by a series of explosions—mysterious detonations that seemed to come from a clear sky. Twenty minutes later, the whole region was shaken by an even bigger bang. About the same time, several bright, luminous objects were seen racing across the sky. They travelled at incredible speed and in complete silence. Many other people witnessed strange flashes and glows around the horizon.

Eyewitnesses in Orting, not far from the scene of the

crash, told investigators that the C-118 had appeared overhead at about 7:45 P.M. All the aircraft's four engines had stopped—and a large chunk of its tail was missing. And, strangest of all, the C-118 was being followed by a formation of three shining discs. Every now and then, one of them would break away and dart towards the transport, skipping over it or veering off to one side at the last moment. It was just as though the C-118 were being hounded by a pack of vicious dogs. Several people in the Orting area watched the aircraft and its unearthly companions until they were out of sight.

A minute later, two bright flashes ripped the sky to the northeast. It was at that precise moment that the radio transmission from the C-118 ceased abruptly with the pilot's frantic, "This is it!"

The first rescue teams to arrive at the scene of the crash found a nightmare of charred, twisted metal fragments—hardly any of them more than a foot across—scattered over a whole mountainside. They found three mangled, dislocated bodies, too—sunk deep in the ground by the fearful impact. The fourth body was never found. There was no sign of the plane's tail fin and rudder. They were found much later, miles away in the hills to the north of Mount Rainier.

From the wilderness of torn wreckage, the accident investigators were able to reconstruct exactly how the C-118 had hit the ground, and they came up with a number of facts that baffled them completely. For a start, they calculated that even if the aircraft had nosedived into the ground under full power, the impact would not have been great enough to rip the machine into such a widely scattered sea of small fragments. But the C-118 had not plowed into the earth nose-first; it had struck on its belly, as though a giant hand had slammed it out of the air with incredible force—just as a person swats a fly.

What happened in those last fateful minutes before the C-118's plunge to earth? Is it beyond the realm of possibility that the aircraft was used as the object of a deadly game of cat and mouse by alien craft—a game that ended in disaster when "they"—whoever or whatever they were—tired of what might have seemed a cumbersome toy and slapped it casually out of the sky?

Killer Sound Waves from the Sky

One grey February day in 1965, a flock of pigeons winged over the woods near Warminster in England's rural Wiltshire. Suddenly, the winter calm was splintered by a vibrant high-pitched hum that came, as witnesses later testified, "out of the sky."

As though struck by some giant fist, the birds faltered in mid-air, struggled to regain formation, and then fell, like a shower of stones into the trees below. Every pigeon was dead, killed apparently instantaneously by mysterious waves of sound.

There was a government investigation, but no scientific theorizing could explain away the attacks on both animals and humans from something violent and invisible in the sky. The file is still open.

It began in the early hours of Christmas Day, 1964, when people were jerked abruptly from their sleep by strange, frightening noises above the rooftops.

A witness said later: "There were crashes, thuds and clatters, as though someone was bombarding the houses with gigantic rocks—and in the background was a high-pitched hum, vibrating on the frosty air."

But outside in the darkness, nothing could be seen, although stone walls shook with echoing vibrations.

Then suddenly, the noises stopped. Puzzled and alarmed, the people of Warminster went back to bed. Some blamed the army: there was a military camp near Warminster. But the army didn't usually carry out exercises on Christmas morning, and the mysterious sounds did not remotely resemble explosions.

The sonic bombardments lasted for six hours on that memorable Christmas morning. No one could come up with a reasonable explanation. But the noises seemed to have died away—for good, it was hoped.

Then, in February, 1965, the sounds from the sky began again, with another strange mid-air massacre of pigeons. And this time the attacks began to take a vicious turn.

One person who felt their full fury was a 19-year-old farmer who was walking along a dark, deserted road after seeing his girlfriend home. The night was silent, all sound blanketed by dense fog.

At first, the youth didn't take much notice of a faint humming noise. Then it swelled into a shrill, ear-splitting screech, "as though all the devils in hell had been let loose."

All at once, a fearsome, bone-crushing pressure clamped down on the young man, forcing him to his knees in the road. An icy, stinging wind tore at his face, and noiseless waves of inexplicable pressure buffeted his body. His head felt as though it were held in iron clamps. Then the pressure lifted, as suddenly as it had descended, and he staggered home. His parents took one look at his white, terrified face and sent for the doctor, who treated the young man for severe shock.

Animals suffered most severely from the assaults. After one weird burst of ultra-sound, dozens of field mice were found lying dead in a field. Their fur was singed and their bodies perforated with tiny holes. Dogs and cats became ill, and canaries and budgerigars toppled dead from their perches.

The violent sound attacks lasted—on and off—until the end of June, 1965. Scientists and government investigators arrived at Warminster and the surrounding area to study the phenomenon and came away baffled.

Is there any rational explanation? Were the sound waves that battered Warminster a product of natural causes—or something else?

And can it be pure coincidence that the place in Britain where the greatest number of corroborated UFO sightings have occurred is Warminster?

Did Michael Norton Fall Through a Hole in Time?

One of the most uncanny stories I have ever come across concerns the baffling disappearance of a Canadian farmer's son, 12-year-old Michael Norton, on a November morning over 60 years ago. The hunt for the missing child went on for years, because although he disappeared physically, both his parents and hundreds of investigators all heard Michael's voice—calling faintly from the same few square feet of ground.

On the day it happened, Michael overslept. When he rushed down to breakfast, he was seen by his father and mother, an aunt, and two farm workers. A few minutes later his mother watched him trudge towards the cow shed. She had no way of knowing that neither she nor anybody else would ever see the boy again.

Some hours later, wondering about his absence, Ruth Norton called Michael to come back to the house or he would be late for school. Michael's younger brother and sister were impatiently waiting for him to take them into the village.

There was no answer to Mrs. Norton's call and, with some irritation, her husband put on his boots and went out to fetch the boy. When he entered the barn, it was empty. The stool and bucket were there, the latter half full of milk. Michael had obviously stopped in the middle of his work—but there was no sign of him.

Mr. Norton searched the barn. He found nothing. He called his family and the workmen and they combed the farm and its environs. There was no trace of the boy.

Seriously alarmed, Mr. Norton drove into the nearby township of Burtons Falls and alerted the police. A few hours later, the police arrived at the farm with a bloodhound, which was given Michael's scent. The animal's keen nose soon detected Michael's trail. It led from the kitchen door into the barn and then out of the barn again, straight into the open south pasture, a field visible from both the house and the nearby road.

Then the bloodhound, which had been tugging excitedly at the leash, suddenly stopped in its tracks. They were in the middle of the pasture, several dozen yards from the farther boundary. Surprised, the handler urged the dog on, but the animal just whined. The trail had disappeared!

What happened? No one ever found out. Search parties were organized and other tracker dogs brought, but none of them ever uncovered a hint of the boy's movements after he had stood in the middle of the field. Michael Norton had literally disappeared into thin air!

A few nights later, when hope of finding their son alive was fading, the Nortons were overjoyed to hear a voice outside. It was Michael's, and it called one word that no other boy would call in that place: "Mum!"

They rushed outside, shouting with relief, and then

stopped. There was no one there! The voice called again, "Mum!" It was Michael, both were certain of that. But they searched and searched and found nothing. They called his name and he didn't answer. Half an hour later, as they stood in the farmyard, peering hopelessly into the dark, they heard him again: "Mum," and this time he clearly added, "Where are you?"

Many people came to the little farm, and many of them heard the lost voice as it called and pleaded for help. One of the most logical theories that was put forth suggested that he had tumbled into an underground river, an old well, or simply a crack in the ground. But this idea was eventually discarded when experts studied the terrain. A primitive form of aerial photography was also used, hoping to pinpoint a fault in the field. But there was no evidence to suggest such a thing.

For weeks, the frantic parents and others heard the disembodied voice of Michael Norton, which was growing fainter as the days passed. It seemed that he was in a thick mist, but quite free to move. Then, after a while, he was heard no more.

Is it possible that some unknown physical law opened a "gap" in time, through which Michael fell or was pulled? And that such a suspension of the normal laws would be visible to the human eye, maybe as a "mist," or some other alteration of the light?

Might it be this disturbance that Michael saw? Might he have run across the field to see for himself, and been swallowed up in the middle of the pasture, which was, for a brief moment, the "eye" in the needle of time?

Death Watch

From the time John Phillips entered the hospital in September, 1952, until his death a few months later, the hospital staff at St. Olive's, in the town of Biddeford in Devon, England, became increasingly alarmed by strange events surrounding the patient. Phillips was an old man in his late 70s, terribly confused and incapable of carrying on a sensible conversation.

Often, under the ward's dim, orange night lights, the atmosphere would appear to be alive and full of movement around John's bed—like heat waves, wavering and fluctuating. But it was the soft persistent *voices* that sent the night nurses rushing out of the ward in terror. Each time anyone investigated to find out who was talking to Phillips, the old man was always fast asleep. And when any of the staff crept up to the bed to listen to the voices, which were always indistinguishable, the noise would stop—abruptly.

A student nurse received a severe reprimand from the night nurse when she reported that she had heard a large animal padding around the ward, but when the older nurse approached the ward, she too heard the clicking of claws on the hard, polished floor.

When she called for help, two doctors and a night porter rushed into the ward to catch the animal, but a thorough search revealed nothing.

Over the next few weeks, nurses often turned up the main lights, crawled about on all fours, and peered under the rows of beds in an attempt to track down the animal. Often the swift, stealthy padding appeared to brush past them. And then they would hear heavy breathing and smell a strong animal odor.

Patients frequently heard the creature also, and many asked that Phillips be removed to a private room. But because of a shortage of beds, this was not possible. The hospital board finally dismissed the footsteps as being either rats running under the flooring, creaking timbers—or just plain imagination.

On a Wednesday morning, 12 days after Phillips had been put in the ward, there came a manifestation that could not be rejected so easily.

Two young nurses were startled to see a head peeping out from behind the heavy, lined curtains drawn across the window at the head of Phillips' bed. The features were those of a young man with dark, curly hair, and they had never seen him before!

Since visitors were not allowed in the wards at six in the morning, the nurses hurried to the window, and as they did, the head withdrew and the curtains fell together again.

The curtains were still moving as one of the nurses pushed them open, but nothing was there—except the closed window, securely locked from the inside.

The screams of the second nurse brought the medical

staff to the ward from all parts of the hospital, and again a thorough search was made without anything being discovered.

It was a closely locked ward. The outside windowsills were about nine feet from the ground, and beyond that was a 12-foot wall topped with iron spikes and a thick ledge of glass splinters.

How could any intruder withdraw his head and shoulders and disappear within seconds, closing and locking the window from the opposite side?

Later the same day, after an emergency meeting, Phillips was removed to a private room. Two experienced nurses were assigned to him. Shortly after one in the morning, both nurses heard voices from within the private room, but every time they checked, Phillips was sound asleep and no one else was present.

Two hours later, they distinctly heard a loud chuckle, and to their horror saw a face protruding from between the curtains of the only window in the room.

The description given by the nurses was the same as that of the person who had been seen before. As they stood rooted to the spot, the face laughed and then vanished.

The window, again, was securely locked. One of the nurses noticed that the temperature of the room had dropped considerably, although the radiators were so hot that it was impossible to touch them with bare hands.

Less than three hours later, John Phillips died. Never again did anyone in the hospital report hearing the strange murmuring voices, the animal sounds, or seeing any mysterious visitors.

4. HORROR BEYOND REASON

- A family returns after a 10-day absence to a house that has gone berserk.

- A room sighs, glows, and pulls people inside it.

- A vicious tree crushes its victims.

The Dark Evil That Haunts Walsingham House

It was difficult to say just when the Walsingham family realized that there was something different about the house—something evil. Certainly, it was before they went in and opened the shuttered windows.

They hadn't been away that long. It was only 10 days since Howard Walsingham had left the house with his wife, their teenage son and daughters, and cat and dog—to visit with relatives and attend a wedding in Charleston, South Carolina, over 100 miles away.

Their farmhouse, which lay on the outskirts of the small town of Oakville, had always been a happy one. But on this spring day in 1889, everyone felt that something was wrong.

The dog, Don Caesar, refused to enter the place. When young Howard dragged him in, he broke into furious snarling and barking. His back bristled with rage. This happened several times. As the day went on, he continued to act strangely, as if terrified.

Later, after a neighbor and his wife came to welcome them home, Walsingham heard whines and growls from one of the rooms. When he went to investigate, he saw that Don Caesar seemed to have gone mad. The big hound leaped into the air as if going for a man's throat, but suddenly he fell back, as if he had received a heavy blow, and lay motionless on the floor.

When Walsingham picked up the dog, its neck had been broken. It was dead.

That evening, around dusk, the house was suddenly filled with shouts and hideous laughter. This was heard by everybody, including the neighbors, and it put them all in a state of near-panic.

Then Amelia, the older daughter, brushing her hair in front of a mirror, plainly saw a man's hand resting on her shoulder. But there was no reflection of it in the mirror, nor any sign of an arm or body.

Walsingham, in the garden, saw footprints forming on the dust of the path in front of him as he walked. Yet nothing mortal could be seen.

As uncanny and terrifying as these events were, they paled into insignificance before the incident that took place later that evening.

The family and neighbors were sitting at supper when loud, terrible groans started coming from the room above. The sounds stopped, and talk began again, until someone remarked on a stain of what looked like blood on the white tablecloth. Young Howard then pointed to the ceiling. A liquid was slowly dripping down onto the table from a patch of red. It was so like fresh blood that they couldn't finish the meal. Instead, they watched, horrified, as the liquid continued to drip. It occurred to them all that some terrible deed, some ghastly murder, was taking place upstairs.

Walsingham raced upstairs, followed by his son, and flung open the door, dreading what he might see. But the room was empty.

Pulling up the carpet, they found the floorboards soaked with the same red, gruesome liquid that was dripping into the room below. But there was no explanation.

After an uncomfortable night, Walsingham rode into Oakville and gave a sample of the liquid to the local doctor, who examined it under a microscope. It was unquestionably, he said, human blood.

These incidents were too much for the Walsinghams, who soon moved to another side of town.

Questioned about anything unusual that might have taken place before the macabre events, Walsingham did remember one incident. The day before the family left for the wedding, a farmhand asked Walsingham to look at a pile of old dried bones that had been turned up by the plow. Not able to decide whether or not they were human, Walsingham ordered them thrown into a limekiln.

A spiritualist group suggested that the spirit of the man whose bones were treated to such an indignity might have summoned dark forces to his aid to make the place uninhabitable by mortals. It seems unlikely that a pile of dried bones could produce such terrifying phenomena. But, as yet, no one has come up with a better explanation.

Room of Sighs

It seemed such a peaceful, comfortable old place, the house in County Down, in Northern Ireland—and so it was. Except in one of the upstairs bedrooms.

My grandfather, Cecil Macklin, rented the house in July of 1912. A few days after moving in, he was shaving at the mirror in his bedroom when he heard it for the first time.

From somewhere within that room, from a few feet behind him, he heard a loud, shuddering sigh. Yet, when he glanced around, there was nobody there.

At first, he thought he had imagined the whole business. Then he heard it again. But he chose to ignore it. He had an idea that his children were playing a joke on him.

So when he left his room, he crept silently along the passage to his children's bedroom and whipped the door open. To his amazement, the children were all fast asleep.

Of course, he didn't mention the incident to anyone, since he still wasn't sure he had heard anything. But within the next few days he heard the sighing again. It always happened during the evening.

Soon, he noticed that the servants in the house came up with all sorts of excuses rather than enter the room, but when he questioned them, all they could tell him was that something there frightened them.

After that, he decided to investigate the phenomenon for himself. He went up to the room in the afternoon and sat in the rocking chair reading. As evening crept down from the mountainside, he became aware of a coldness that filled the room.

Determined to wait for the sighing to begin, he stayed in the chair until it was too dark to read. Then he heard it again. And it almost terrified him out of his wits. For the moaning and sighing seemed to boom out right in his ear, and he realized that it was coming from the chair in which he was sitting!

Springing up, he stared at the chair that was now rocking wildly. Then, all at once, something even more weird happened. The chair stopped rocking—almost as if some invisible hand had halted it!

The heavy sighing was still behind him, and as he moved across the room to light the lamp, it followed him. Suddenly, all his courage deserted him and he rushed for the door—the moaning and breathing pursuing him all the way, until he had wrenched the door open and slammed it behind him.

But as he leaned against it and turned the key in the lock, he could quite clearly hear *something* snuffling and grunting on the other side of the door.

For the rest of the summer the room was kept locked and none of the family ever went in there again.

But the haunting didn't stop at that.

Some weeks later, when weekend guests were staying at the house, two of the men walking outside saw a strange, pinkish glow coming from the window of that room.

They dashed into the house, shouting "Fire!" and rushed up the stairs. The room was locked, but a strange smell was coming through and they could see a bright light beneath the door.

It was a stout, heavy door, and they couldn't smash it down, so one of the men hurried down the stairs to get an ax. Just as he returned to the top of the stairs, the door flew open. The other man cowered back in horror as a pink light blazed forward. Then a shadow blotted it out and two strong, muscular arms came from the room, pulled him inside, and slammed the door shut.

There was a scream, and the second man began crashing the ax down on the door panels. My grandfather joined him and they forced the door open. They found the room in darkness—and their friend lying unconscious on the floor. They carried him out—and behind them, something sighed—a heavy, despairing sigh, that neither wanted to investigate further!

When their friend came to, he couldn't say what had happened to him. All that he remembered was the door springing open and a dazzling bright light blinding him for a few moments before somebody pulled him into *a dark room*. Then he fainted.

In the morning, everybody left that house—forever, as it turned out—and spent the rest of the weekend in a nearby inn.

None of the local people were surprised by their vacating the house. What was surprising was that it had only been a few months earlier that the house had first achieved the reputation of being haunted. Before then, it had been occupied by the same family for over 200 years, and during that time it had been a happy home.

Then, early in 1912, after it had been sold, it was being renovated. One of the workmen was alone in that bedroom, plastering part of the wall. Suddenly he heard a sigh.

At first, he thought it had been caused by a draft, or the wind outside. Then he realized that it was coming from within that very room—from a few yards away—but there was nobody there. Nothing, except the shadows dancing in the flickering light from his lamp.

But what made the flame flicker? There was nothing to explain it.

Then the rocking chair, which had been absolutely motionless until that moment, started to sway gently back and forth, exactly as if somebody were sitting in it.

From then on, the workmen refused to go into the room except by twos, and then only in daylight.

The house is still there, and it's still occupied, but the people living there don't use the room except to store their unwanted bits and pieces. And the door is still kept locked.

Killer Tree of the Cameroons

All that was left of the campfire was a smoldering glow deep in the wood ash, but Bob Fellows, huddled snugly in his sleeping bag beneath the old tree, didn't notice that, in the last few moments before the African dawn.

Something had roused him from his sleep, and for a moment he lay there wondering what was wrong. Then he heard a rustling noise from the tree above his head, and a few moments later, a weird, gurgling moan. Thinking that there might be a leopard or some other animal about to attack, he snatched up his flashlight and rifle and turned to waken his partner, Mike Cura.

That was when he saw it. Mike Cura's sleeping bag had been ripped to shreds and there wasn't a sign of him. Then something whipped through the darkness and smashed against Fellows' shoulder.

The blow sent him spinning across the ground and half stunned him, but a choked scream brought him to his senses. The cry came from up among the branches of the tree, and training his flashlight on them, Fellows saw a horrifying sight.

His partner's body was being slowly and powerfully crushed to death by the branches of the tree. One branch had wrapped itself around his throat and was strangling him, while several other, thicker ones were exerting such pressure on his body that Fellows could almost hear the bones splintering.

Then, slowly, when the life had been squeezed out of the victim, the grotesque killer tree unraveled its branches and let Cura's body fall limply to the ground.

Fellows remained where he was, too horrified and too frightened to move, as the uncannily arm-like branches groped blindly towards him. But they couldn't quite reach him.

Fellows stood there until the first streaks of daylight. The tree gave a heavy, shuddering sigh, and its branches seemed to lose their life.

Four days later, in May 1903, Fellows was telling police in Iloku, in the Cameroons, that his partner had been murdered by a tree! Of course, the authorities didn't believe his story. Fellows was held on suspicion of murder, while an expedition set out to recover Cura's body.

When the body was brought back to Iloku, an inquest was held, but the results of it were so startling that they were not made public for many years. Fellows was, however, freed from jail and the charge was quietly dismissed. For the doctors who carried out the postmortem stated that Fellows *could not* have killed his friend; the damage had been inflicted by some powerful, *super-human* creature. One doctor said that he doubted if even a gorilla would have possessed the strength to mutilate a body so severely.

Shortly afterwards, a missionary working in that district heard about Cura's death and wrote Iloku authorities about similar incidents.

Apparently, 12 men had been found dead at the base of that tree within a period of 50 years, and for centuries the African tribesmen had treated that particular stretch of forest as *taboo.*

The origins of the legend were based on a tribal priest about 80 years earlier, a man named Ubo, who suddenly went berserk and started a campaign of terror in the region. Many people were waylaid by him and strangled to death for no reason at all.

At last the warriors set out to hunt the killer down. They trapped Ubo beneath the tree one evening during a thunderstorm. As they closed in for the kill, there was a flash of lightning. The tree was struck, and so was Ubo, who had been standing with his back to the trunk. When the tribesmen recovered his body, they found that both his hands had been sliced off at the wrists by the lightning. Yet the warriors couldn't find the missing hands anywhere.

It was soon after that, according to the missionary, that the tree started to gain the reputation of being a "strangler" tree.

But that wasn't the end of the story.

Less than six months after the death of Mike Cura, a boy from the mission school staggered into Iloku to gasp out an incredible story to the police. The missionary had been killed by the tree—right before the boy's own eyes.

The boy had gone with the missionary to chop down the tree and destroy it once and for all. But they hadn't arrived there until late evening, and while the boy started a camp, the missionary approached the tree with an ax.

Even before the blade hit into the tree trunk, the boy heard the missionary scream in terror. He turned just in time to see thick branches wrapping themselves around the man's body.

The police inspector who went to investigate found the dead missionary hanging limply in a fork in the tree trunk. By then it was morning and the tree seemed nothing more than just a dead tree.

However, the inspector and his patrol had instructions to destroy it—which they did. With a loud groan, the mighty trunk crashed to the ground. Then it was chopped and sawed into logs that were piled in a heap to be burned.

Before this could happen, a strange and gruesome discovery was made. As one of the soldiers split a log, he found two human, skeleton hands trapped within the wood. Both hands had been severed at the wrists.

5. UNCANNY!

Steer to the Nor West...

- Did the sacred cat escape from its coffin?

- There is a strange attraction that exists between the hunter and the hunted—even in death.

- Skipper and crew vanish—and then the ship does, too.

- A sleeping man telegraphs a psychic SOS.

The Sacred Cat

His fatal encounter with the mummy case (see "When Death Comes on Swift Wings," page 6) was not the first terrifying situation that archaeologist Gordon Richardson had faced with an object from one of the Egyptian tombs. There had been his spine-chilling experience with the sacred cat.

The mummy of the cat was contained in a small coffin when native workmen brought it out of the tomb of one of the Pharaohs. Why they then put the unopened mummy case in Richardson's hotel room remains a mystery. They didn't tell him about it. And when he returned to his room after dark, he stumbled over the small coffin and nearly broke his neck.

The coffin was made in the shape of a sitting cat and

was in two shell-like sections. Inside would be a mummified cat sitting upright, embalmed and wrapped in cloth.

Richardson left the case where it was. When he went to bed it was still sitting there in the center of the room, staring at him with its painted eyes.

In the middle of the night, he was awakened by a noise like a pistol shot. As he sprang up, a large grey cat sprang across his bed, clawed his hand viciously, and dashed away through the open window.

By the time Richardson recovered from his shock, he was startled to see by the light of the moon that the two sides of the coffin had burst apart and were still rocking to a standstill on the floor. Between them sat the sacred embalmed cat, swathed in bandages.

When he scrambled out of bed, a chill swept over him. The bandages on the mummified cat had been savagely torn open at the throat—as if by an animal clawing its way to freedom.

Richardson knew that ancient Egyptians believed that the souls of the dead left the body by way of the throat. But another idea was forming in his mind—one that belied a lifetime of rational thinking and all his scientific training. He could not help toying with the seemingly preposterous idea that the sacred cat had torn itself free from its bonds—and that the grey cat that attacked him was the mummified cat's escaping spirit.

Of course, Richardson said later, there was a perfectly straightforward explanation for the entire experience. It was possible that the brittle wooden coffin had broken open because of the accidental kick he had given it—and perhaps because of the change of atmosphere from the dry desert to the more humid banks of the Nile.

And the grey cat probably had wandered into his bedroom from the village, possibly through the open window.

And the injury to the embalmed cat's throat? That might have happened when the ancient undertaker, just before sealing up the cat's coffin, stole the jewel that he knew would be there under the wrappings.

Possible? What do you think?

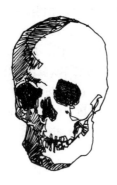

The Hunter and the Hunted

The ghost of an elephant control officer is often seen roaming in the bush in Zimbabwe, some 20 miles from Serenje. It's as if he is still doing his duty: hunting down rogue elephants and keeping them away from the farm country.

Although it was sometimes Richard James's job to kill the great beasts, he made no secret of the fact that he had an enormous respect—even affection—for the elephants.

He frequently spoke of them as the gentlemen of the jungle, wise, courteous and affectionate, and said that when he had to die, he only hoped that he would be killed by an elephant. He got his wish.

On one of his tours from his base at Serenje, he penetrated deep into the bush, chasing a rogue elephant.

When he caught up with it, he hit the elephant with his first shot, but failed to kill it. Then, when the wounded and infuriated animal charged him, his gun misfired.

Everything happened so quickly that his bearers were unable to shoot before the animal reached him and hurled him into a tree.

After the elephant was killed, they climbed the tree and gently brought James back to the ground. They carried him a short way, but his back was broken and he knew he was dying. His final request was to be buried at the spot where he had fallen. He wanted to stay in the bush country forever.

His bearers soon prepared a grave, and after a short burial ceremony made the long trek back to Serenje, where they reported the tragic accident.

The story should have ended there. But when the news of James's death eventually reached officialdom, whoever received it failed to understand the significance of the dead man's request. A month later, a special expedition was sent to exhume his body and take it back to the European cemetery at Mpika, near Serenje.

But when the expedition arrived, the grave was surrounded by elephants. Each time someone moved in the direction of the grave, the elephants became angry and charged.

Two days passed; a number of elephants were killed, and eventually the body was recovered and the expedition went back to Mpika.

John Littler was appointed to be James's replacement, and six weeks after the funeral he heard that elephants in that area were causing a great deal of disturbance and damage. He decided to go back to the place where the accident had occurred, but had great difficulty persuading his bearers to go with him. It was as if they had a premonition of what was about to happen.

The party was within 100 yards of the original grave when one of the bearers gave a terrible scream, dropped the supplies he was carrying, and ran back along the path.

He was quickly followed by all the native bearers. Littler and his assistant stood alone, surrounded by supplies that lay where the bearers had dropped them as they fled.

Then both men saw the cause of the panic. For there, standing near the grave, surrounded by a large herd of elephants, was Richard James.

Littler knew that it could not be James. He had helped to bury his colleague. It had to be his ghost.

Both men moved forward, and as they did, several elephants lifted their trunks, bellowed, and turned as if to prevent them from reaching the grave.

The ghost seemed to wave them back. It was as if he was warning the two men that if they came any nearer they could easily be killed by the elephants, who by now were very angry indeed.

Littler decided to heed the warning, and the two men retreated, leaving the ghost of Richard James with his beloved elephants. Since 1958, many officials and hunters have reported seeing the ghost within a mile of the spot where he was killed.

Was this a classic case of a man "returning" because of a guilty conscience? Or did he possess a curiously involved relationship with his enemy—the strong affinity that so often exists between the hunter and the hunted?

The Riddle of the Seabird

The crowd waited patiently as the sailing ship *Seabird* made her way towards shore. They didn't know it, but they were witnessing one of the greatest sea mysteries of all time.

The *Seabird* was completing a voyage from Honduras to Easton's Beach, near Newport, Rhode Island.

But suddenly, instead of heading for the landing place, the *Seabird* swung off course. Picking up speed, it sailed swiftly towards the long, dangerous reef that lay a mile out. Its sails were full as the ship gathered speed. The crowd gasped, for many boats had met their end on the killer strip of jagged rock.

The skipper must have gone mad, everybody thought

in amazement, as they waited for the inevitable catastrophe.

But there was no crash, no crunching of timber. Just as the crowd prepared themselves for horror on that Sunday morning in November, 1850, they witnessed a miracle. At the very last second, a great swell lifted the ship and swept her clear over the reef. The *Seabird* kept going as if nothing had happened—until she came to rest a few yards from the beach.

For several moments the crowd stood in silence. Then, recovering from their amazement and terror, they cheered. But only echoes answered them. Not a sound came from the ship now floating peacefully in the shallow water.

When no one appeared on deck, some of the bystanders waded out to investigate. When they boarded the *Seabird*, they found only one sign of human life—the captain's dog, a well-fed and affectionate mongrel. The skipper and his crew of more than 30 men had vanished without a trace—and probably only minutes earlier—while the ship was in sight of shore!

A pot of coffee was simmering gently on the stove, and it had not been made long. All the instruments were working perfectly. The skipper had noted in his log book that the ship had passed Branton Reef—just two miles offshore from Newport—within sight of the watchers on shore.

Puzzled and alarmed, the locals called in the police, who found nothing. A blank was also drawn by experts who went over the ship from stem to stern. They could offer no explanation of how a skipper and crew could vanish into thin air in broad daylight in full view of nearly 100 people.

A sea search was organized in the hope that some of the missing crew might be picked up. But none were. At last, orders were given for the ship to be unloaded. As the cargo was taken ashore, careful watch was kept for any clue to what had happened to the crew in the two miles between Branton Reef and the shore. It took four days to unload the *Seabird*—and no ship had ever been emptied more carefully. But still there was no trace of the crew.

Baffled, the police gave up and the experts returned to their various headquarters. A message was sent to the owners of the *Seabird* to send a new crew to take her back to sea.

They never did, for early one morning, exactly one week after she arrived, the *Seabird* vanished, slipping out to sea as mysteriously as she had arrived. Like her crew, the *Seabird* was never seen again.

The Man Who Projected Himself

One of the weirdest and most baffling types of psychic phenomena is the inexplicable power of certain people to project themselves from one place to another. While they remain physically in one place, they may be seen many miles away—appearing, at least, to be quite real.

Perhaps the most extraordinary case was related at sea in the year 1860 by Captain John Clarke, master of the schooner *Julia Hallock*, trading between Cuba and New York. He had heard it from a seaman named Robert Bruce from Devon, England.

Bruce, according to Clarke, was an honest and upright man who would not have lied about anything. He was also a first-class seaman, having risen to first mate by the time he was 30.

Bruce had been serving on a vessel plying from Liverpool, England, to New Brunswick, in eastern

Canada. His strange experiences took place after six weeks at sea. Darkness had fallen and Bruce went to the captain's cabin to work out some navigational calculations.

Bruce, intent upon his figures, did not notice that the captain stepped out of the cabin. When he had arrived at a conclusion, he announced their present longitude and latitude without looking up.

Receiving no reply, he raised his head and was astonished to see that not only had the captain gone, but that a complete stranger was sitting at the writing table.

Bruce was a man of more than average courage, but the sight of the strange man's keen eyes boring into his filled him with sudden apprehension. He did not stop to ask questions but fled and sought out the captain, who was back on the bridge.

Seeing Bruce's white face, the captain commented, "You look as if you've seen a ghost."

Bruce said: "Who is that man sitting at your desk, sir—in your cabin?"

The captain stared. "There is no man in my cabin—and if you saw anyone you must be seeing things, Mr. Bruce."

When Bruce insisted that he had seen a strange man, the captain suggested that it must have been another crew member.

"It was not, sir—I know every man in the crew well enough to know that this man was a complete stranger to me," Bruce insisted.

The captain, realizing his mate was in earnest, ordered Bruce to go back to his cabin and ask the stranger to step up to the bridge. But Bruce was afraid now, without knowing precisely why. He said he would rather not go back to the cabin alone.

At first the captain was angry and ordered Bruce not to be ridiculous. Finally he went down to the cabin with Bruce. It was empty. But then they both saw some writing on the captain's slate. The words were: *Steer to the Nor'West.*

The captain called to the cabin every man who might have entered it on some duty or other, and made each in turn write out the same words. None matched the writing on the slate.

"Do you believe in ghosts, Mr. Bruce?" the captain asked.

Bruce said he did not.

"Nor do I believe in such things," said the captain. "But all the same, I think we will sail that way—just to see what does happen."

In the middle of the next afternoon, the lookout reported sighting an iceberg. When the captain and Bruce trained their glasses on it, they saw a vessel trapped in the ice.

The ship was a schooner on her way from Quebec to Liverpool with about 60 passengers. Water and food were dangerously low. The crew and passengers were in a sorry plight. Had Bruce's ship not sailed that way, all might have died of starvation and exposure.

Bruce was on deck supervising the rescue operation when one man in a very weak condition was hoisted aboard. Bruce went to assist him, and when the passenger lifted his head, Bruce recognized the face.

It was the very same man he had seen sitting in the captain's cabin—miles from that spot!

When he was feeling stronger, the passenger was asked to go to the cabin and write on the slate the words *Steer to the Nor'West*. He did so, and the writing was found to be exactly the same!

The passenger obviously could not have written the message, trapped as he was on the ice-bound ship. And when asked, he said that he did not recall even having a dream in which he wrote such a message.

But the captain of the wrecked vessel reported that at the hour when Bruce saw the stranger in the cabin, the man had been in a very deep sleep. When he awoke, he had said something strange: "Captain, we shall be rescued very soon now—by sunset tomorrow at the very latest."

And the passenger went on to tell the captain that he had dreamed of being aboard a strange ship that was coming to the rescue. He even described the ship in detail as he came out of his deep, trance-like sleep— although he did not remember the dream ten minutes later.

The description, which the captain remembered distinctly, fitted Bruce's ship exactly.

6.
ENCOUNTERS
WITH GHOSTS

- The perfect model—this beautiful woman wears a black ribbon around her neck.

- A victim of the blizzard disappears—again and again.

- A psychic vision is also an omen of disaster.

Portrait of a Ghost

It was the summer of 1913, and Lebrun, a promising young artist, had only been in Paris for a few weeks. A shy man, especially in the company of women, it took some courage for him to speak to the young girl he saw standing beneath the street lamp in Montmartre. She was looking about her so helplessly—so obviously uncertain of her whereabouts—that Lebrun finally decided to go to her assistance.

She turned towards him—and his first reaction was astonishment, because he had never seen a more beautiful face! And instead of offering to assist her, he found himself begging her to pose for him.

For several moments she stared at him with a puzzled, frightened expression in her eyes. Then, slowly, she replied:

"A portrait would take several sittings and my time

here is very short. Tonight I am with you—but tomorrow I have no idea where—"

Lebrun resolved to finish the painting in one night, and he pleaded so hard that she finally nodded and walked along silently beside him.

When they reached his studio, he set to work at once. She was a perfect study in black and white; her face had a pale, almost deathly hue about it and her clothes were coarse and black. She had a black band high on her throat, and when Lebrun asked her to remove it, she stared at him in terror—and shook her head.

As Lebrun worked through the early hours of that morning, the girl sat perfectly still, perfectly silent.

The first cold light of the new day was over the horizon when Lebrun finished painting. It was a perfect likeness, except for the black band, which he had decided not to incorporate into the picture.

The girl left without even saying goodbye. Lebrun hurried after her, but she had disappeared into the early-morning gloom. And apart from the sound of her footsteps dying away in the distance, it was almost as if she had never existed.

Later that day his landlady came to the studio to collect Lebrun's rent. She took one look at the portrait on the easel and exclaimed, "What a good likeness of Gretel Pederson! You must have seen her photograph in the papers after she was guillotined for murdering her parents and her husband."

Lebrun stared at her. He hadn't heard about the murder and surely had not seen the girl's photograph.

After pacing his room for hours, he decided that he must have been overworking. The whole thing must have been a figment of his imagination—he must have glanced at her photograph in the papers and somehow it had registered in his subconscious.

Just as he was deciding to take things easier, he heard a knocking at his door. It was Julien Sant, an artist friend.

"Lebrun, you can call me a madman if you like—but last night I saw a ghost!"

Sant went on: "It was early evening, about eight o'clock, in the streets near here. There was a young girl and I was obsessed by the thought that I had seen her somewhere before. I just saw her as I passed, but I could never forget that beautiful face.

"Today I went along to the newspaper files, and I saw her photograph. It was Gretel Pederson!"

Lebrun said nothing. Instead he pointed to the picture.

"That's her, all right," said Sant. "But when I saw her she had a high black band around her throat."

Sant added, "And that's not all. I found out that last night was the anniversary of her *death*. . . !"

The Corpse That Walked Away to Die Again

The fiercest blizzard Scotland had known for over 50 years had been raging for almost four days in February, 1963, when Joe Turnbull's truck ran into a snow drift high on the remote Beattock Summit in Lanarkshire. There were hundreds of other vehicles abandoned along the road.

Turnbull realized that if he stayed where he was, it might be days before he was reported missing, and by then, it would be too late. So he set out to walk to the nearest village.

The whirling snow, hurled at him by a biting cold wind, made it impossible to see more than a few feet in front of him. That was why he didn't see the body lying facedown in the center of the road until he stumbled over it.

Slowly, Turnbull freed the body of a bearded young man from the freezing snow and wrapped his red, brightly patterned scarf around the head to protect it from the cold. The man appeared to be dead.

Turnbull wasn't sure about that, though, and he couldn't walk away and leave the man lying there, because if he weren't dead, he soon would be.

Lifting the unconscious man onto his shoulders, Joe started trudging through three-foot-deep snow drifts to Beattock village. It was almost two miles away, but now *two* lives depended upon his succeeding.

Some time later, when he was almost fainting from exhaustion, he heard voices and saw the gleam of flashlights. To his relief, two men came striding through the snow. When they saw him almost on his knees with the body across his shoulders, they hurried to assist him.

The darkness, the thickly falling snow, and their hooded jackets hid their faces, but as they took the unconscious—or dead—man from Turnbull, they exchanged details.

They, too, were truck drivers, they said. And when Turnbull explained about the body, they offered to take it with them to a railway station a few miles across the fields. Turnbull was invited to accompany them, but since he could see the lights of the village, he decided to press on.

Then the two strangers, carrying the limp body between them, disappeared into the storm. And disappeared is the only word to describe what followed. For neither the truck drivers nor the "corpse" were ever seen again.

Joe Turnbull reported the incident to the police, but when they checked with the trucking companies the two strangers were supposed to work for, they found no record of any people with those names ever having been employed. As the storm slackened off, police launched a search for the two men and their burden.

There was always the danger that they had all perished in the blizzard, but no bodies answering their descriptions were discovered. And no men had reached the railway station either that night or in the 48 hours afterwards.

Then there was the scarf that Turnbull had wrapped around the "corpse's" head. It had still been there when the other men carried him off, but during the intensive police hunt all over the moors, the scarf was never recovered.

But it *was seen* again! A motorist who had abandoned his vehicle a few hours later that night, several miles on the other side of Beattock village, later told police how he and his wife had met a young man answering that description. He had been bearded and was wearing a *brightly patterned red scarf around his head!*

The three of them had walked together towards the village, but somehow during the height of the blizzard, the young man had fallen behind. And although they called out to him and hunted back along the road for a few hundred yards, they failed to find him again.

Soon afterwards people started reporting a ghost on Beattock Summit—the ghost of a young, bearded man wearing a colorful scarf around his head. The man stands at the roadside trying to thumb a lift from passing cars. Whenever a car pulls up, the young man vanishes.

Herne the Hunter

Arnold Beckett's favorite place was Windsor Great Park. There was nothing he liked doing better than strolling for hours through the magnificent forest. Soon, he came to know practically every inch of the area.

One autumn twilight in 1931, when Beckett was about to make his way back to the station to catch a train home to London, he realized that there was something different about the park. There was something different especially about the clearing he had walked through a few moments earlier. For in the center of it was a huge tree—and he was sure that he had never seen one there before.

Beckett stopped and stared at the tree for a long time, wondering if he had perhaps confused this clearing with some other. But he was so convinced that there had been *no* tree there that he began to feel quite nervous.

Then, as he walked around the tree, he saw something horrible and grotesque. Hanging from a lower limb, a corpse was swaying on the end of a rope!

His first instinct was to cut the man down, but as he hurried forward to do this, his feet sank into the long grass and he stumbled on a loose branch. To keep from falling on his face, he threw his hands forward to break his fall.

His eyes couldn't have left the tree for more than a split second, and yet, when he looked again, there was nothing there. No hanging man and no tree.

Beckett's heart raced with fear. He had no idea what was happening, but he knew that he wanted to get away from that place as fast as he could!

For a time he kept his strange experience to himself. But later he did tell what had happened, and then he learned from a schoolmaster in Windsor that what he had most likely seen in the forest had been the ghost of Herne the Hunter.

Herne the Hunter had been a forest warden when Henry VIII was on the throne—but more than that, he was said to have practiced witchcraft under a certain tree in the park. And it was from that tree that Herne had hanged himself. For centuries his specter had been known to haunt the forest and it had been seen many times before.

His appearance, however, was a certain omen of disaster.

Beckett was fascinated by the legend, but he remained skeptical about the appearance of the ghostly tree being an omen of disaster.

Then six months later, after Beckett's business unexpectedly failed, he committed suicide. He hanged himself from a tree in Windsor Great Park.

7. SKIRMISHES WITH THE SUPERNATURAL

- A witch doctor draws a line.

- A Ouija board dooms four party guests.

- The most astounding premonition of all time forecasts the very moment of death.

Demon Tree

A lot of people didn't like the tall, powerfully built Dutch civil engineer Jan Bekker, for he was a pretty hard character and he had stepped on a good many toes. But everyone admitted that whatever his faults, Bekker was a determined man who got things done.

It was just before World War II and Bekker was in charge of a construction unit, composed mainly of native labor. He had been hired to build a road along the mountainous west coast of Sumatra between Cota Raja and Sibolga. There had been the usual snags, but work was going ahead according to plan.

One morning, Bekker received two visitors—the headman and witch doctor of the village—both in a state of agitation. Bekker managed to make out that they wanted him to alter the road's course in order to avoid a grove of tamarind trees, the next target for Bekker's bulldozers. The men said that the trees were taboo—and that the tallest one was the home of a demon named Subarjo, who would bring down a terrible vengeance on anyone who disturbed him.

Bekker had heard some of his men murmuring fearfully and now he gave a loud snort of anger. Facing them, he bellowed: "I fear neither man nor demon. And to prove it, I am going to pull down those trees—starting with the biggest one!"

Unlike the headman, whose face was contorted with fear, the witch doctor showed no emotion. He stared impassively at Bekker for a few seconds, then picked up a stick and drew a line on the earth across the road's intended course.

"Your road will not be built beyond this point," he said calmly, then turned and strode away.

Bekker ordered his men to fasten a chain around the biggest tamarind and attach it to one of the heavy tractors. Slowly, the big machine began to take the strain—and at that moment there was a loud, vicious crack. Bekker ducked just in time to avoid the broken end of the chain. It went whistling past and smashed the skull of one of the laborers.

At the same instant, a scream of agony rang out. The tractor had veered to one side and crushed a second workman under its tracks.

While the men were being buried, the witch doctor and the headman returned. "Two lives have already been lost because of the wrath of Subarjo," the witch doctor said. "Once again I must ask you to leave his spirit in peace and to turn the road aside."

Bekker's patience snapped. "Now, listen," he shouted, "my job is to build this road—and I'm going to do it on time and as planned, even if I have to uproot every blasted tree in Sumatra!"

Bekker's men were terrified by this time, and it took a great deal to persuade them to return to work. But eventually they went back.

Once again, chains were fastened around the tree and the big tamarind creaked and groaned as the tractors took the strain. An electric, fearful atmosphere hung over the spot as the men watched breathlessly. To them—and to Bekker, too—it seemed as though the tree was fighting back, resisting the pull of the tractor with uncanny strength. But at last it gave a loud groan, as though of despair, and came shuddering up out of the earth. And as it did so, the workmen recoiled in sheer horror.

For there, entwined firmly among the roots, was a human skeleton.

Even Bekker was taken aback—but only for a moment. Striding forward, he surveyed the pitiful bones—and then turned to face his men. "There is your demon—no wonder he could not rest in peace. Look— he is pierced through by the roots. Take these bones and bury them somewhere else in a quiet place where he will no longer be in torment. We start work again on the road in the morning."

When he finished speaking, Bekker noticed that his men seemed relieved. Some of them were even smiling. He turned to see what effect his words had on the witch doctor, but the man was gone.

Bekker had an uneasy feeling, though, that his victory had not been as complete as he might have wished.

Even so, he wasn't prepared for the shock that awaited him the following morning. At the exact spot where the witch doctor had drawn his line in the dust, the ground was split by a chasm several yards in length and three feet in width. Other smaller cracks radiated outwards towards the grove of tamarinds. The entire surface of the ground was scarred with them. And they were natural—not man-made—as Bekker suspected at first.

How or why the cracks had appeared, literally overnight, was beyond Bekker. He only knew that he could never build his road straight through the tamarind grove now.

The tamarind grove still stands, and the road that Bekker built curves around it in a wide loop that the local inhabitants call Subarjo's Bend. And a few yards from the trees, the bones of Subarjo himself lie still, peaceful and undisturbed, in the spot where Bekker laid them.

The legend of the demon tree has been forgotten.

Partying with the Ouija Board

It was a frosty February night in 1963, and many of the guests had come to the party in Norfolk, England, from towns as far as 50 or 60 miles away. Four had come a mere 30 miles. These four discovered at 11:30 that night that they had been selected to die.

It was a Ouija that gave the message. All that is needed for a Ouija is a board that shows the letters of the alphabet in a semi-circle, as well as the words "Yes" and "No," and a light wineglass. To work it, the operator positions the glass upside down in the center and touches the base with one finger. Presumably, the spirits of the dead channel enough energy into the glass to move it across the table to spell out messages or answer Yes or No.

The Ouija board had become the fad of the moment. The usual light-hearted questions were asked and the glass rumbled around, giving obedient answers.

Mike Chambers, who had just joined the group, was

worried about driving home. Addressing the air above the table, he asked, "What sort of road conditions will there be?"

After a pause, the glass gave a surprisingly clear answer: *Ice patches . . . bend.*

This direct message inspired more questions: "How far away?" *Many miles.* "Will there be an accident?" *Yes.* "Will anyone be killed?" *Four people . . . people four.* Then the glass appeared to lose interest and meandered around the board. But the group was fired with a morbid interest.

"What is the nearest landmark to the accident?" *Marsham Arms.*

The Marsham Arms was an inn midway between Norwich and the little fishing town of Sheringham, where the party was being held. Furthermore, it stood on a bend near a crossroads, fulfilling other factors the Ouija had noted.

Two more questions were asked that would set the seal of doom on the four people. The first was "What time is this accident to take place?"

After much wandering and slithering, the glass spelled out *One o'clock.*

Mike Chambers had already decided to get home by 1:30, which meant he had to leave the party by 12:15. He realized that, if he followed this schedule, he would be rounding the bend on which the fateful Marsham Arms stood at just about one o'clock.

Hardly knowing that he was asking the clinching question, he dumbly watched the glass move to *Yes.* His question: "Will anyone in this room be involved?"

Since Mike's car was the only one going in the direction of Norwich, it was obvious to everyone in the room that he and his friends were the ones referred to by the wineglass.

The party had died. As the guests filed out the door, one of them turned and said to the hostess: "Why not keep Mike and the others back a little longer? That way they won't be near the Marsham Arms when the accident is supposed to happen."

It seemed such a good idea that Mike was glad to agree. He started out exactly an hour after he had intended to leave.

During the homeward journey, the prophecy was apparently forgotten. But not for long. Rounding a bend a few miles from Sheringham, Mike's small car skidded wildly. In a shaky voice, one of the girls said, "Phew, ice patches, just like *it* said."

Heedful of the ice menace, Mike drove more slowly. At last they came to the rise that overlooked the Marsham Arms Inn.

The car radio was playing a pop tune. The road, as they gazed down at the sleeping inn, descended at a shallow angle until, curving left, it ran onto the crossroads. The ice on it glittered in the moonlight.

There had been no accident that night. There were no skid marks, no wrecked cars.

As they entered the wide bend, the music from the radio stopped. An announcer's voice came over the air.

"This is the American Forces Network, Frankfurt," the voice said. "The time is now exactly one o'clock Central European time."

As he spoke, Chambers and his friends saw the headlights of another car flashing past the stark trees that lined the road. The car was moving too fast to round the bend with the ice they *knew* to be on it.

Reg, sitting behind the driver, said it. "It really *is* one o'clock! We forgot, the clock goes *back* for winter!"

At that time the British still kept up their wartime practice of moving the time backwards or forward an hour in winter and summer. The four realized that one o'clock in Germany was in reality one o'clock in England, not an hour later as their clocks said.

The oncoming car, a Jaguar, roared over the crossroads directly in their path. Someone shouted, "Brake—for God's sake!"

Mike knew better. "I can't!" he cried. Braking on that treacherous surface would throw the car into an uncontrollable skid. There was only one way to slow down, and it was only slightly less dangerous. Mike double declutched and changed gear from fourth to second. The engine howled, the gears screamed, and the car shuddered as its forward motion was slowed by its own engine going slower than the wheels it drove.

At that moment, the other car hit the ice. Its front slipped around, headlights glaring. The massive hood of the Jaguar swung around and pointed towards them. Swift as a bullet, it slithered across the road, hit the bank mere feet in front of them and bounced clear. Then it bounced again briefly before plunging its gleaming snout once more into the scarred earth.

At that moment, Mike's car crept forward through the gap between the bank and the Jaguar, as the other car bounced off. Mike cleared it, just as the giant sports car lunged forward and hit into the space where Mike's car had been seconds before. Had it hit their flimsy car, they would have been steamrollered. Surely, they all would have been killed!

Those are the facts. The direful prophecy was fulfilled in most ways: There were ice patches and there was certainly one outside the Marsham Arms. There was an accident and it did involve four of the people at the party. It took place at one o'clock. *But no one was killed.* The other driver merely suffered a concussion.

How much had reading the future altered it? If he had not known of the future accident, Mike Chambers would have left at the time he originally intended, not an hour later. But having been alerted, he took a risk with his car that he would not normally have taken. He said later that had it not been for the warning, he would have expected the other driver to slow down in time.

Of course, there is another question, and it is real and ominous. Is it certain that the accident was due to happen on the night of the party? Or might it take place on some frosty night in the future . . . ?

You Will Die at Midnight

Probably the most amazing case ever recorded of a death premonition concerned Thomas, Lord Lyttelton.

The remarkable events took place in November, 1779. Lyttelton had gone from London to his country house in Epsom, where he was convalescing after an illness. Walking in the large conservatory with Lady Affleck and her two daughters, Lyttelton noticed a robin perched on an orange tree close by. He tried to catch it, but failed. Seeing the ladies exchange amused glances, he vowed he would catch it—even if it killed him. After a long chase, he succeeded.

The next morning, Lyttelton appeared at the breakfast table, so pale and haggard that his guests anxiously asked him if anything was the matter. Finally, he told them a strange story.

The previous night, after he had lain awake for some time, he heard what sounded like the tapping of a bird at his window, followed by a gentle fluttering of wings in his room. Puzzled, he raised himself on an elbow and saw an amazing sight. In the center of the room stood a beautiful woman dressed in white, with a small robin perched like a falcon on her wrist. This woman told him to prepare for death as he had only a short time to live. When Lyttelton was able to speak, he asked how long he had. The phantom replied, "Not three days. And you will depart at the hour of 12."

For two days Lyttelton fluctuated between despondency and hysterical gaiety. At dinner on Saturday, the third day, he amazed his guests with his wit and vitality. But afterwards, he lapsed into a gloomy silence, and as the evening wore on, he grew restless. He could not sit still but paced restlessly to and fro, muttering incoherently. Every few minutes he took out his pocket watch, gazed at the time, and wiped beads of sweat from his forehead.

Eventually, when the hands of his watch read half-past 11, he went to his room, without a word of farewell to his guests. He had no idea that not only his own watch but every clock in the house had been put forward half an hour by well-meaning friends!

Sitting up in bed, watch in hand, Lyttelton awaited the fatal hour of midnight. As the minute hand slowly approached 12, he asked to see his valet's watch and found that it showed the same time as his own.

With pounding heart and straining eyes he watched the minute hand draw nearer and nearer midnight. A minute to go—half a minute. Then it pointed to the fatal hour—and nothing happened. It crept slowly past. The crisis was over!

Lyttelton put down the watch with a sigh of relief,

then broke into wild, hysterical giggling. He spoke to his valet for ten minutes more and seemed to be his normal self once again, completely at ease.

Then he remembered his nightly dose of medicine and asked his valet to prepare it. As no spoon was at hand, the valet stirred it with the handle of a toothbrush that lay on the bedside table. Lyttelton scolded him for his dirty habits and ordered him to fetch a proper spoon.

When the servant returned a few minutes later, Lyttelton was lying back on his pillow, breathing heavily and with a strange, haunted look in his eyes. The valet ran downstairs to get help. The alarmed guests rushed to his room, but a few moments later, he was dead, the watch clutched in his hand pointing to half-past 12. In reality, he had died on the very stroke of midnight.

Index

12292